Happy 24th Kelly!

Love

Your "New" Mom

courtesy of

Dr. Sclesinger!

Cal's Aloha Recipes

A Teenager's Family Cookbook

Calera Uchigakiuchi Schlesinger

INSPIRE

(An Adducent nonfiction imprint)
Adducent, Inc.
www.Adducent.Co

Titles Distributed In
North America
United Kingdom
Western Europe
South America
Australia

Cal's Aloha Recipes

A Teenager's Family Cookbook

Calera Uchigakiuchi Schlesinger

Cal's Aloha Recipes

A Teenager's Family Cookbook

Calera Uchigakiuchi Schlesinger

ISBN 978-19375923-4-9

Published by Adducent (under its Inspire nonfiction imprint) in the United States of America
Jacksonville, Florida

www.Adducent.Co

This publication is an informational product based on the author's own experience and experimentation to develop the recipes. The author has taken efforts to convey her recipe ideas correctly and to review each recipe carefully. Sometimes you may not get the desired results due to various factors like quality of products, variations in ingredients, time taken in cooking and individual cooking ability. Before trying ANY recipe, read the recipes and most importantly, be sure that you like the ingredients. Of course you are free to make modifications to any recipe to your tastes. All statements of fact or opinion expressed are those of the author and don't reflect the official positions or views of the publisher. Nothing in the contents should be construed as asserting or implying authentication of information or endorsement of the author's views. This book and subjects discussed herein are designed to provide the author's opinion about the subject matter covered and is for informational purposes only.

Dedication

I dedicate this book to
Sacred Hearts Academy.

Next to my family, Sacred Hearts has been the cornerstone of my existence.

I will be a Daughter of Sacred Hearts Academy (SHA) which is an honorary title bestowed upon young women who have completed continuous enrollment from Kindergarten through graduation from high school. When I graduate, I will have been at Sacred Hearts for 15 years because I started in pre-pre Kindergarten.

Sacred Hearts is an exceptional institute of learning in Honolulu, Hawaii.
It is in the Kaimuki district, and Ms. Betty White has been our Head of the School since before anyone can remember.

Like all students, I have had my ups and downs during these past 14 years, but I would not be the good student and the creative person that I am today without the encouragement and loving attention that I received from all of my teachers, counselors and administrative staff at Sacred Hearts Academy.

Many SHA personnel deserve to be named in this dedication,
but the one person I truly want to single out was my lower school dean and counselor,
Ms. Toni Gopaul,
who unfortunately passed away before she saw me receive my diploma.
She was instrumental in helping me survive the lower grades before my parents discovered that my learning disability was not due to a lack of intelligence,
but was due to ADD and dyslexia. Ms. Gopaul was always supportive in spite of what appeared to be my inattentiveness, and I would not be graduating from Sacred Hearts Academy next year without her loving intervention.

Thank you Ms. Gopaul and everyone at Sacred Hearts.

"Queen of Hearts"

"My Queen of Hearts is my edgiest painting. The Queen shows attitude because she is the Queen, and as we know, if she wishes, it would be off with your heads."

Introduction

Calera Uchigakiuchi Schlesinger, known to her family and friends as "CAL", is the adopted child of an entrepreneurial Mom and an artistic, cosmetic plastic surgeon Dad. She attends a Catholic girl's school, Sacred Hearts Academy in Honolulu, and has studied Shotokan karate for the past seven years. Cal has a cat named Burt and the sign on her bedroom door is "The Swamp" for good reason.

She is also an artist and loves to paint. Cal and her father, Larry, love the story of Alice in Wonderland, her beloved grandmother's name was Alice, and Cal's collection of paintings and recipes is an homage to her Mongolian roots and her adopted family. She and her mother, Arlene, love to cook. especially for friends and family. Cal also loves photography and took all the photographs of the recipes for this book.

Cal's pride in being creative extends to the kitchen, especially when things don't work out quite the way the recipe said it would. AS WITH ART, SO IT IS WITH FOOD! It's very important to think creatively – and Cal's creativity has transformed meals from "doubtful" to "delicious". Through that experience, she has devised her own unique modifications to recipes in order to take a simple "meal" and turn it into a special time with family and friends.

Since in Hawaii, family is everything, Cal wanted to share some of her simple, yet delightful recipes with other teenagers so they too can cook for their families.

You're holding the result in your hands!

"White Rabbit"

"My White Rabbit was painted as a friendly, loving character perfect for kid's bedrooms, dedicated to the tea party, and since tea time in England is 4:00, it is 3:30 and he has to hurry so as not to be late."

Why the Alice in Wonderland Paintings?

I remember my Popo (Grandmother in Chinese)

who I loved very much. She passed away in February, 2012.

Her name was Alice.

It was not her given name at birth. She was born into a family of six boys and six girls.

Her four older sisters were not allowed

to continue their education past the eighth grade but had to work to earn

money for the family. My grandmother was fortunate to have the

opportunity because of the kindness of the headmaster of a private boarding school to

attend high school. She wanted to have an English name and chose

Alice from the book, "Alice in Wonderland".

My grandmother was a remarkable woman. She started high school when she was 18

years old, earned her RN degree during World War II, and went back to college when

she was 55 years old to complete the Bachelor's Degree she

started but did not finish at the University of Hawaii.

In honor of my Popo, I have painted in watercolor, some of the characters from the

books by Lewis Carroll.

"Alice"

"In this painting, Alice is pondering all her adventures in Wonderland, yet she is not quite sure what they all mean which is symbolized by her mouth being a question mark."

Table of Contents

"Caterpillar"

"My Caterpillar is smoking a hookah, sitting upon a magic mushroom, appears to be Mongolian Chinese, and asks the question of Alice (as a stoner would), "Whooooo are yooooou?"

Beef
&
Pork

Aunty Carole's "Easy"
Asian Barbecue Pork Ribs

Preparation and Cooking Time: 2½ hours

Serves: 4

For Sauce:
- ❧ 4 tablespoons hoisin sauce
- ❧ 1 tablespoon light soy sauce
- ❧ 2 teaspoons Shaoxing wine (Chinese rice wine)
- ❧ 1 teaspoon kosher salt
- ❧ ½ teaspoon Chinese five spice
- ❧ 2 tablespoons water
- ❧ ½ cup sugar

For Ribs:
- ❧ 3 ½ lbs baby back pork ribs

The First Step:
Preheat oven to 325 degrees. Cut each slab in half, arrange in roasting pan, and bake for 1 hour without any sauce.

The Final Step:
Continue baking ribs another 1½ hours, this time with the sauce. Brush sauce on ribs, then brush every 15 to 20 minutes until done. Alternate between top and bottom sides in the baking.

To Serve:
Slice into individual ribs pieces to plate.

Cook's Tips:

Except for the baking time, you can make this dish really fast. It is good for a family dinner, but is also a no fail dish when you are having friends over. It makes a good pupu (appetizer) for a party.

Cook's Notes:

When I was younger, I spent a lot of time at my Aunty Carole's house. Both she and Uncle Neil are great cooks, and I loved everything they made. My Uncle Neil is an artist with the camera. Photography is his hobby but he definitely could have been a professional – he is that good! When I told him I was interested in photography, he let me have his Leica camera which was his first professional grade camera. He showed me how to use it and gave me advice on lens, lighting, shutter speed, framing, and focusing. I hope I did him justice with the photographs I took for my book.

Aunty Carole would tell me I could have cooking lessons when I reached her shoulders. Since she is so petite, I reached her shoulders in the 5th grade and was still too young for lessons. We call her the Martha Stewart of Hawaii not only because of her incredible cooking, but because she is a perfectionist when it comes to presentation and table settings. She gave me inspiration, not only to learn, but to practice, innovate and excel.

Whenever we tell her how delicious something was, she would always say, "It was easy"! Aunty Carole, now this is what I call easy!!!

Ms. Gopaul's Meatballs with Tomato Sauce

Preparation and Cooking Time: 1 hour
Serves: 6

The Meatballs:
- 2½ lbs. ground beef
- 1 egg
- 4 slices white bread soaked in milk then broken into bite-sized pieces
- ½ cup grated parmesan
- 2 teaspoons kosher salt
- Freshly ground black pepper
- 1 small onion and ½ cup Italian parsley chopped fine and sautéed in olive oil before adding to meat mixture

The Sauce:
- 1 28-oz can whole tomatoes in a large bowl and mashed with your hands
- 3 garlic cloves minced
- 2 5.5-oz cans V-8 juice
- 15 fresh basil leaves
- 1 teaspoon kosher salt

The Garnishes:
- Parmesan reggiano freshly grated
- Italian parsley finely chopped

Making Sauce:
Heat a medium size saucepan on medium high heat. When pan is hot, add 1 Tablespoon olive oil and garlic to pan. Be sure you don't burn the garlic. When garlic is lightly browned, add the rest of the ingredients and cook uncovered on low heat for around 20 minutes.

Making Meatballs:
Heat a small pan on medium high and sauté onion and parsley until softened. Transfer to a dish to cool slightly. Mix all ingredients in large bowl. Use hands to mix, but do not squeeze or compress anything, being careful not to overmix. Heat large pan on medium high. When pan is hot, add 2 Tablespoons olive oil. Brown meatballs on all sides and remove to platter. Use paper towel to clean pan, then return meatballs to pan, add sauce, and cook on low heat for about 20 minutes.

Cook's Tips:

This dish is the one that got me started cooking. Aunty Carole would make us meatballs to take home. I really enjoyed her meatballs and wanted to learn how to make them at home. My first time was a success which gave me motivation to want to learn more.

Cook's Notes:

This recipe is dedicated to my elementary school dean and counselor, Ms. Toni Gopaul. She passed away three years ago from cancer. This is a comfort dish for many people, and Ms. Gopaul was very comforting to me. I have many fond memories of her. There was a period when I was not doing very well in school, and Ms. Gopaul was my advocate. She stood by me, gave me very valuable advice, and let me know that I could come to see her anytime I needed to. I can still hear her say, "Hi, Calera" whenever she saw me on campus. I miss her.

I am not the only one who misses her. Ms. Gopaul was loved by the students and faculty. Her spirit was warm, she really cared for others, and she must have made a great difference in many peoples' lives because when we had services for her in the school gym, there were many people there with flowers in honor of her memory.

Jasmine's Mexican Pork Stew

Preparation and Cooking Time: 2 hours
Serves: 4

The Stew:

- ❀ 2 lbs. boneless pork butt or shoulder cut into 1" cubes
- ❀ 2 garlic cloves finely chopped
- ❀ 1 onion chopped
- ❀ 1 green bell pepper chopped
- ❀ 2 plum tomatoes chopped
- ❀ 1 14 oz. can diced tomatoes
- ❀ 1 16 oz. jar mild salsa
- ❀ 1 7 oz. can Mexican green chilies
- ❀ 2 bay leaves
- ❀ 1 package Lawry's taco seasoning
- ❀ 2 teaspoons kosher salt

The Garnishes:

- ❀ Rice
- ❀ Sour cream
- ❀ Cilantro chopped fine
- ❀ Avocado cubed (optional)

Preparing the Stew:

Heat large pot on medium high heat. When hot, add around 2 Tablespoons canola or olive oil. Add pork in batches and brown on all sides. Add onion, garlic and green pepper to pot with pork and cook until vegetables softened (about 5 minutes). Add tomatoes, salsa, chilies, bay leaves, salt, and taco seasoning with 2½ to 3 cups water. Bring to a boil then turn heat to low. Simmer, stirring occasionally so bottom doesn't burn, for 1½ hours or until pork is tender.

To Plate:

Using a shallow bowl, put one serving of stew over rice. Garnish with cilantro on top and a dollop of sour cream and scoop of cubed avocado on the side.

Cook's Tips:
This one is a great weekend family meal. I say weekend because of the cooking time. The preparation time is fast, but it has to cook on low heat for over an hour and this is what makes it a hard one for the weekdays. If you have family or friends over for dinner, this is a "no fail" dish to make.

Cook's Notes:
One thing I know about my friend Jasmine is that she loves Mexican food. With other foods, she takes awhile to eat, but when it's Mexican, she eats it fast! With her love of Mexican food, I figured I would make something she would like, so here it is! Jasmine and I have been friends for a very long time. She is very energetic, friendly, and funny. She does some of the weirdest things that make me laugh, like the time she wore a horse head, dressed like a hippie, so she was a hippie horse for Halloween. She also makes funny faces and says some of the weirdest things like, "I'm a wolf-frog". Her favorite animal is a frog, but where the wolf comes from, I have no idea. Only Jas knows.

Aunty Sarah's Mexican Stuffed Bell Peppers

Preparation and Cooking Time: 1½ hours
Serves: 4

For Beef Stuffing:
- 1½ lbs. ground beef
- 1 large round onion finely chopped
- ½ cup chopped cilantro
- 2 garlic cloves minced
- ½ cup cooked long grain white rice
- ½ cup canned black beans
- ¾ cup shredded Mexican cheese blend
- 1 package mild Taco seasoning
- 1 16-oz jar tomatillo salsa
- 1 egg beaten
- 1 teaspoon kosher salt
- Freshly ground black pepper

For Peppers:
- 4 large red bell peppers

The First Step:
Preheat oven to 350 degrees.

Preparing the Peppers:
Cut off top ½" of peppers and scoop out seeds. Discarding the stems, finely chop the pepper tops.

Preparing the Stuffing:
Heat large skillet on medium high heat. When hot, add 2 Tablespoons olive oil and sauté ground beef until it just starts to turn pink. Add onions, parsley, chopped peppers, and garlic. Cook around 8 minutes or until onions are softened. Add taco seasoning, salsa (reserve ½ cup of salsa to use as topping), salt and pepper. Continue to cook another 2 to 3 minutes to meld flavors. Transfer to a large bowl, then add rice, beans. Toss together, adding first egg then cheese (save some cheese to use as topping).

Fill pepper cavities with the beef mixture and arrange in a baking dish. Top each pepper with the remaining salsa and some cheese. Put ¼ cup water in bottom of the baking dish, cover with foil, and bake until peppers are tender and filling cooked through (around 45 minutes).

Cook's Tips:

The first time I made this dish, I didn't put water in the bottom of the baking dish. This turned out to be a mistake because the stuffing cooked, but the peppers were still crunchy. As a serving idea, shred some iceberg lettuce, make a fresh salsa (with chopped tomatoes, cilantro, scallions, and lime juice), and a dollop of sour cream to serve on individual plates with the peppers. It makes a great accompaniment and completes the meal with a salad.

Cook's Notes:

I dedicated my Mexican stuffed bell peppers to Aunty Sarah because the presentation with the colorful bell peppers is strikingly attractive just like her, but the spicy filling is such a delightful surprise to the palate like her strong and spicy personality. Both the bell peppers and Aunty Sarah are eye candy but take no prisoners.

Uncle Jason's New York Steak Burgers

Preparation and Cooking Time: 45 minutes
Serves: 4

The Burger:
- 1 ½ pounds New York steak (sometimes they sell this in thin slice at lower prices)
- Maldon sea salt flakes

The Fixings:
- 4 slices Swiss cheese
- Shredded iceberg lettuce
- 4 tomato slices
- Buns of your choice

The Dressing:
- 1 cup mayonnaise
- ¼ cup ketchup
- ½ cup cornichons diced

The Tools:
- Kitchen Aid mixer with meat grinder attachment

The First Step:
Get all the fixings and dressing ready and set aside. If using a gas grill, start to heat to high. If using a grill pan, can heat on high heat as soon as you grind the steak.

Cut the steak into cubes and put through the grinder. Use some cubes of bread to get the last of the meat out of the grinder. Divide into four portions and form patties making a depression in the middle. Sprinkle both sides with Maldon salt to your taste. Add the cheese to the tops of each burger during the last minute of cooking. As soon as the meat is done to the temperature you want, remove to a plate.

Put buns on grill to toast both sides. Be careful not to burn the buns as they heat up quickly. Believe me, I have burned many a bun.

To Assemble:
Put a generous amount of dressing on both sides of the bun, then add the burger, tomatoes and lettuce.

Cook's Tips:

It's amazing how much the New York steak flavor comes through in the ground meat. I was so surprised that the burger tasted just like a New York steak – it was absolutely delicious. You must try this one! My Aunty Carole made it for us the first time, and we just had to make it for ourselves so we went out to buy the meat grinder attachment for our Kitchen Aid. It was one of the best things we bought.

Cook's Notes:

I dedicate my New York steak burger to Uncle Jason because it has both soft, melodic flavors along with the strength of prime New York steak. My Uncle Jason is strong and somewhat imposing due to his large earrings and shaved head and height, but then again, he loves good food, especially meat and although he would not admit it, he has some soft melodic tones to his personality as well. This burger looks like any other burger, but when you get to know it, just like Uncle Jason, it is very high quality!

Uncle Eric's Skillet Ground Beef Pie

Preparation and Cooking Time: 1½ hours
Serves: 4

First Layer:
- ❀ 2 lbs. ground beef
- ❀ 1 large round onion finely chopped
- ❀ 3 carrots peeled and finely chopped
- ❀ 8 cremini or white mushrooms chopped
- ❀ 1 Tablespoon fresh thyme leaves
- ❀ ¼ cup flat leaf parsley finely chopped
- ❀ 1 Tablespoon tomato paste
- ❀ 1 Tablespoon flour
- ❀ 1¾ cups beef broth
- ❀ 2 teaspoons kosher salt
- ❀ Freshly ground black pepper

Second Layer:
- ❀ 8 small Yukon gold potatoes
- ❀ 2 Tablespoons butter
- ❀ ½ cup sour cream
- ❀ ½ cup milk
- ❀ 1 teaspoon kosher salt
- ❀ Freshly ground black pepper

Third Layer:
- ❀ 1½ cups grated cheddar cheese
- ❀ 1 cup scallions finely chopped

First Step:
Preheat oven to 350 degrees.

Preparing Pie:
Heat 1 Tablespoon olive oil in large cast iron skillet. Brown beef until no longer pink, removing to a dish as soon as it turns color. Add onions to pan and sauté until onions light brown – around 5 minutes. Add chopped carrots and cook another 5 minutes. Add mushrooms, tomato paste, thyme, and parsley, cooking for around 2 minutes. Stir in flour and mix in well. Add beef broth, salt and pepper. Return meat to the pan, cover, turn heat to low, and simmer for about 25 to 30 minutes or until liquid is gone.

In the meantime, bring small pot of water to boil, add potatoes, lower heat, and cook for around 20 minutes. When potatoes done, drain water using a colander, return potatoes to the pot, cover with cloth to absorb steam, and let sit for 5 minutes. Mash the potatoes either with a masher or fork, add butter, sour cream, milk, salt and pepper.

When meat done, spoon potato mixture over meat to cover. Sprinkle with cheese followed by scallions. Put pan in oven and bake uncovered for around 20 minutes. It is done when top is crusty and golden.

Cook's Tips:

This dish is really a simple one to make, especially if you do it in a pan. It is fast and by the time you finish all the steps, your dish is ready to serve. All you need is a salad on the side for a complete meal.

Cook's Notes:

This one makes me think of Uncle Eric, my Mom's business partner. I think of England and Ireland with this dish, and Uncle Eric is a good golfer and went to Ireland and Scotland to play, part of his "bucket" list according to Mom. She also calls these trips his spa trips because he comes back so healthy and fit from walking all those long courses everyday. This also feels like "down home" food, and I feel at home with Uncle Eric because we did a lot of things together when I was younger. He would call me "banana" all the time. He has a daughter, Jena, who is one year older than me. We took a lot of fun trips together to the neighbor islands, including a lot of pool time, water slides, camping, swimming with the dolphins (which I nearly blew by not obeying instructions), and ziplining.

Sacred Hearts Academy
Taco Pizza for Friends

Preparation Time: 45 minutes
Serves: 4

The Ingredients:
- 2 readymade 12" pizza crusts
- 8 oz. can Mexican refried beans
- 2 teaspoons Tabasco or Frank's Red Hot
- 8 oz. jar pizza sauce
- 1 lb. ground beef
- 1 package Lawry's taco seasoning
- 1 cup black olives sliced
- ½ cup scallions thinly sliced
- ½ cup green bell pepper chopped
- 8 oz. Mexican blend shredded cheese

The Garnish:
- 3 plum tomatoes chopped
- Iceberg lettuce shredded

First Steps:
Preheat oven to 400 degrees. When oven comes to temperature, cook pizza crusts until just done – around 6 to 7 minutes.

In a small bowl, mix refried beans with hot sauce. Heat medium size pan on medium heat. When it comes to temp, brown ground beef until it just turns pink. Add taco seasoning, cooking for another minute, then remove from heat.

The Assembly:
Layer pizza in this order: pizza sauce, refried beans, ground beef, olives, scallions, bell peppers, then cheese.

Bake for 8 to 9 minutes or until cheese is melted. When done, remove from oven, top with chopped tomatoes and iceberg lettuce.

Cook's Tips:

Don't skip the tomato and lettuce garnishes. When I first made this pizza, it looked so good already, I thought about not using it. I tasted the pizza with and without, and boy, did the tomato and lettuce add freshness and took it to another level. This is a great one when friends come over. Everyone will just love it.

Cook's Notes:

When I graduate high school, I will be a "Daughter of Sacred Hearts" because I will have a total of 15 years as a student there. In fact, I will be among the first to have 15 years because I was in the very first pre-pre Kindergarten class offered. Prior to that, they only had Junior and Senior Kindergarten. I feel very fortunate to be attending Sacred Hearts Academy. The faculty and administration are all willing to help the students. They are friendly, kind, dedicated, and most of them are very easy to talk to. The campus is small but beautiful and clean. We recently built a new Art Center and just completed a new cafeteria that we call the Student Center. I have enjoyed and appreciated every one of my teachers through all my years. They are tough, they don't make it easy for you, but they are also very nice and you can go to them if you need help anytime. I called this recipe "Sacred Hearts Taco Pizza for Friends" because many people there are truly my friends.

Uncle Shimo's Pork Chops with Pea "Smashed" Potatoes

Preparation and Cooking Time: 1 hour
Serves: 4

The Pork Chops:
- ❀ 4 pork chops
- ❀ 2 eggs beaten
- ❀ 1 cup flour
- ❀ 1 cup Panko (Japanese breadcrumbs)
- ❀ ¼ cup Italian parsley finely chopped

The Mashed Potatoes:
- ❀ 3 small russet potatoes
- ❀ 2 Tablespoons butter
- ❀ ½ cup milk
- ❀ 1 cup frozen peas
- ❀ 1 teaspoon salt
- ❀ Freshly ground black pepper

The Garnish:
- ❀ 1 lemon cut in wedges

Making the Potatoes:

Peel potatoes, then cut each potato into 4 pieces and add to medium size pot filled halfway with water. Bring water to boil, lower heat, and simmer for around 20 minutes or until potatoes done. Blend milk and peas in blender and put in small pot.

When the potatoes are cooked, drain in a colander, return to pot, mash with a fork, and cover. Start heating milk and pea mixture on low temperature. When warm, add butter and pour over potatoes. Add 1 teaspoon kosher salt and black pepper. Cover to keep warm.

Making the Chops:

Set up station with 3 bowls. In one bowl, put eggs and 2 teaspoons water, mixing well. In second bowl, put flour, and in the third bowl, put Panko and chopped parsley.

Heat a large skillet on medium high heat. Salt and pepper pork chops, then coat with flour, knocking off excess. Dip into egg and coat with Panko. When pan hot, add ¼ cup olive oil and start cooking pork chops on medium high heat. You may turn down heat if the chops start burning or browning too quickly, and you may have to add more olive oil while cooking. Pork chops will take about 6 to 7 minutes to cook.

Cook's Tips:

Don't over blend peas because you want to have peas in small chunks, not pulverized. Also, be careful not to make your pan too hot for the pork chops, otherwise the coating will quickly burn. Don't be afraid to add more oil as you cook the chops. As long as your pan maintains the temperature, adding oil will not make the chops greasy.

Cook's Notes:

There are a lot of foods that my Uncle Shimo doesn't like (actually, it's easier to name the things he likes since that is a much shorter list). However pork is definitely one of his likes. Uncle Shimo is my personal trainer and a good family friend. He is a famous Hawaii mixed martial arts fighter who started as a boxer, and smashing is part of his job. I purposely smashed the potatoes with a fork instead of using a potato masher. I felt I was smashing him back for all the pain and suffering he puts me through with the pushups, burpees, leg raises, squats and lifts. Uncle Shimo, take this!

Hulali's Italian Sausage
Paccheri With Tomato Cream Sauce

Preparation and Cooking Time: 45 minutes
Serves: 4

The Sauce:
- 4 Italian sausages (2 hot and 2 mild), casings removed and crumbled
- 1 small round onion finely chopped
- 1 clove garlic minced
- 1 25 oz. bottle tomato basil sauce
- 1 cup frozen green peas
- ½ cup basil torn
- ½ cup milk (can be 1%, 2% or whole)
- 1 teaspoon kosher salt
- Freshly ground black pepper

The Pasta:
- ¾ lb. paccheri or rigatoni

The Garnishes:
- 1 cup freshly grated parmesan reggiano
- ¼ cup fresh basil chiffonade

The First Step:
Bring large pot of water to boil. Just before adding pasta to boiling water, add 2 Tablespoons kosher salt. Cook until pasta al dente (around 10 minutes), then drain in colander. Retain 1 cup pasta water for use later.

To Make Sauce:
While pasta water heating, start making the sauce. Heat large skillet on medium high with 2 Tablespoons olive oil. Once oil is hot, start browning sausage, and when the sausage is halfway cooked, add onions and garlic. Continue to cook for around 5 minutes then add tomato sauce. Simmer for another 5 minutes, then add basil, peas and cream. Immediately add drained pasta to the pan. Toss to thoroughly mix together, bring up to temperature, adding some pasta water if too thick.

To Plate:
Transfer pasta to a serving bowl or to individual serving bowls. Top with grated parmesan and basil.

Cook's Tips:

If you like your pasta creamy, you can mix the grated parmesan with some ricotta and put a dollop on each serving. Also, if you can, get your Italian sausage from Whole Foods. I think they have the best.

Cook's Notes:

Italian food is one of Hulali's favorites. She especially loves pasta prepared in any style with any sauce. Most of the time, whenever I see her lunch, it is some kind of pasta. I am sure she would like this if I made it for her! Hulali is one of the kindest people I know. She may be a little socially shy at times because she is not comfortable meeting new people, but she has a heart of gold. She is a great friend to talk to if you have any problems because she is a good listener.

Uncle Kirby's Slavonik Style Steak Marinade

Preparation and Cooking Time: 5 hours (includes marinade time)
Serves: 4

The Marinade Ingredients:

- 4 ribeye steaks 1½" thick or 4 fillet mignon steaks 12 oz. each
- 1/3 cup rum
- 3 Tablespoons sweet wine
- 1 Tablespoons onion grated
- ½ teaspoon dried oregano or 2 teaspoons if fresh
- ½ cup olive oil
- 1 teaspoon kosher salt
- 1 large garlic clove grated
- 1 package Schillings or McCormick's meat marinade

In a mixing bowl, whisk marinade ingredients together. Marinate steaks in refrigerator for at least 4 hours. Grill on charcoal or gas grill to desired temperature.

Cook's Tips:
You will be surprised how good this marinade is on Spencer or Ribeye steak. For some reason, because the Spencer has more fat and the texture is not as firm as a filet, the absorption is better and the taste is unbelievable. This goes real well with a stuffed baked potato.

Cook's Notes:
I am not sure where this recipe came from. It has been passed down in our family for two generations, and all I know is, it makes real tasty steaks. It is also good for kabobs. Slavonik sounds Russian, so I think of Alaska and Uncle Kirby. I think of Alaska because they have a lot of Russian names in their geography including the town of Seldovia where my Uncle Kirby and Aunty Lynn live. Uncle Kirby is a real tough guy and he likes meat, that's why this is for him. He is also a real fun guy. When he comes to Hawaii, he takes me kayaking and we always have a great time no matter what we do.

 # *Aunty Louise's Yummy Raisin Sauce for Baked Ham*

Preparation Time: 30 minutes

The Sauce:
- ❀ 1 cup golden raisins
- ❀ 1¼ cups water
- ❀ 1 cup light brown sugar
- ❀ 1 Tablespoon butter
- ❀ 1 Tablespoon apple cider vinegar
- ❀ 1 Tablespoon lemon juice
- ❀ 1½ Tablespoons Worchestershire sauce
- ❀ 5 whole cloves
- ❀ 2 teaspoon cornstarch
- ❀ ¼ teaspoon paprika

To Prepare:
Combine all the ingredients in a small saucepan and simmer for 20 minutes.

Cook's Tips:

This is another one passed down from Popo. Since my father likes raisins, I decided to try it one day, and he really liked it.

Cook's Notes:

Aunty Louise works with Mom. I think of her with this sauce because Aunty Louise doesn't like sauce on anything. She will not eat rice or any starch if it is "wet" meaning there is sauce or gravy on it. It doesn't matter how much or how little – it has to be "dry". I think she might try this sauce as long as it is only on the ham and nothing else, and I think it probably has to be "golden" raisins, not the regular ones, just like her.

"Door Mouse"

"My door mouse is a child-like, friendly, benign character who sits in a Wedgewood teacup to indicate his proper English roots."

Chicken

Cousin Ted's Korean Buffalo Wings with Cucumber Salad

Preparation and Cooking Time: 1½ hours
Serves: 4

The Marinade:
- ❀ 2 pounds chicken drummettes
- ❀ 1½ cups soy sauce
- ❀ 1½ cups brown sugar
- ❀ ¾ cup scallions finely chopped (use both white and green parts)
- ❀ 3 cloves garlic crushed
- ❀ ¼ cup sesame oil
- ❀ ¼ cup toasted sesame seeds

The Batter:
- ❀ 1 cups flour
- ❀ ¾ cup cornstarch

The Cucumber Salad:
- ❀ 2 stalks celery thinly sliced on the diagonal
- ❀ 2 Japanese or English cucumbers thinly sliced
- ❀ 2 radishes thinly sliced
- ❀ 1 Tablespoon kosher salt
- ❀ 1 Tablespoon fresh ginger slivered
- ❀ ½ cup rice wine vinegar
- ❀ ½ cup sugar

To Make The Chicken:
Combine all ingredients and marinate chicken for at least 45 minutes. Heat 3 inches canola oil in a heavy bottom deep skillet or pot. Need to reach frying temperature of 350 degrees. Mix flour and cornstarch on a plate. Coat chicken with flour mixture dusting off excess and fry.

To Make Cucumber Salad:
While chicken marinating, make the salad. Put the sliced celery, cucumber and radishes in a bowl with the salt and toss. After 20 minutes, thoroughly rinse and squeeze excess water before removing to a small bowl. Add the vinegar, sugar and ginger and mix well. Keep in the refrigerator until ready to serve.

Cook's Tips:
Be sure your oil is not too hot because it will burn the coating but the chicken will not be cooked. I throw a sprinkling of flour in the oil to test the temperature. Using both flour and cornstarch in the coating makes the wings crispier. As the wings are done, transfer to a wire rack. Do not put on paper towels as it will get soggy.

Cook's Notes:
Eating chicken wings the cleanest was a competition between Ted and me. We would compete to see who ate them the cleanest (bone practically shining). He would win most of the time because he loved chicken wings so much, so this is for you, Ted! I challenge you!!!

Ted and I spent a lot of time together at Popo's house. We would climb trees, play basketball, plant a vegetable garden, help with yard work, wash dishes, go to the movies, go to the beach. I loved being with Ted and miss him since we don't see each other that often any more.

My cousin is a champion Yu'gioh card player. He competes in tournaments and recently won the "regionals" in Hawaii where players can qualify to participate in bigger tournaments on the mainland. Last year, he competed in a tournament in Los Angeles and I am sure he did well!

Joe's Lime Marinated Chicken Wings

Preparation and Cooking Time: 3 hours
Serves: 4

For Marinade:
- ❧ 2 cups canola oil
- ❧ 1 ¾ cups light soy sauce
- ❧ ¾ cup freshly squeezed lime juice
- ❧ 1 packet Splenda
- ❧ 8 cloves garlic finely minced

For Chicken:
- ❧ Chicken wings (16 pieces)

First Step:
Mix all marinade ingredients together and add chicken wings. Marinate for 2 hours, turning every 30 minutes.

To Cook:
Grill on either a gas or charcoal grill.

Cook's Tips:

This is another no fail dish that you can make for a family dinner or friends. The key is the marinating time. Because of the canola oil, you do not have to be concerned about over marinating the chicken. It will not be salty and the longer the better.

Cook's Notes:

Joe is like a second father to me. He takes me to school and back, and to all my appointments. He is always there whenever I need him and I depend on him a lot. I feel like I should give something back to Joe because he is so special, so this is my way of showing my appreciation to him.

Joe is from Vietnam, so I used lots of garlic and lime. Joe's wife is a great cook. She makes the best char siu bow, the best fishcake stuffed eggplant and peppers, and the best sponge cake. Sometimes when I am on vacation, they take me to lunch. We go to a Vietnamese restaurant and have some real good pho. Sometimes, Joe buys me some dim sum and chicken feet because he knows this is a real treat for me!

Uncle Danny's Chicken Stew with Mushrooms

Preparation and Cooking Time: 1½ hours
Serves: 4

The Chicken:
- 1 whole chicken cut into 8 parts
- 6 Tablespoons Lawry's Garlic Salt
- ½ cup flour
- Freshly ground black pepper
- 4 Tablespoons olive oil

The Stew:
- 3 cloves garlic finely chopped
- 1 onion cut in cubes
- 12 cremini mushrooms cut in half
- ¼ cup Italian parsley finely chopped
- 2 carrots cut into bite size pieces
- 2 stalks celery cut into bite size pieces
- 2 plum tomatoes cubed
- 4 small Yukon Gold potatoes cut in half
- 3 cups chicken broth
- 1 bay leaf
- 2 Tablespoons ketchup

To Prepare:

Heat large pot on medium high heat with olive oil. Season chicken pieces with Lawry's salt and black pepper, then roll in flour before adding to pot. Brown chicken in batches, being careful not to overcrowd pot otherwise chicken will not brown nicely. Do not turn chicken over too soon or it will stick to the bottom. Add more olive oil if necessary.

When all chicken pieces are browned and removed to a dish, add garlic, onion, carrots, celery and parsley to pot. Cook for around 5 minutes. Add mushrooms and tomatoes and cook for another 3 minutes. Add chicken broth, bay leaf, and chicken, bring to a boil, turn heat down to low and simmer. After 15 minutes, taste for salt adding more if necessary, add potatoes and ketchup and simmer for another 20 minutes.

Cook's Tips:

Stews are liked by most everyone, so is chicken, so the combination is a winner. The essential part of this dish is the browning of the chicken. This is what gives the stew the deep flavor. Also, you can use a lot of vegetables to make it healthy. You can even add, at the very end, cubed zucchini. Don't cook the zucchini but just mix it in about one minute before serving. This will add some crunch to the dish plus another vegetable. I learned this trick from my Aunty Carole who always maintains the texture of the vegetable in her stews and soups.

Cook's Notes:

This dish is simple, yet comforting, just like my Uncle Danny. It is humble, yet it has so much to give. The feeling that I get from this dish is the same feel that I get from him. I think it is fitting that this should be his dish. Whenever we have a Monday holiday, we cook dinner for Uncle Danny. We have travelled the world with these dinners. So far, we had Mexican, Japanese, Chinese, Jewish, Korean, Austrian, Italian. We haven't decided which country is next. Maybe it will be American.

"Mad Hatter"

"My Mad Hatter is a flamboyant, multi-colored personality carrying a half cup of tea and a Wedgewood teapot with the number 4 coming out of the teapot, all of which indicates tea time in England."

Seafood

Aunty Joycelyne's Fish Nachos

Preparation and Cooking Time: 45 minutes
Serves: 6

The Fish:
- 1½ lbs. salmon cut into ½" cubes
- 1½ teaspoons cumin
- 1½ teaspoons dark chili powder
- 1 teaspoon kosher salt
- ½ teaspoon garlic powder

The Nachos:
- 1 large package tortilla chips

The Filling:
- 1 8 oz. can black beans drained and rinsed

- 2 plum tomatoes finely chopped
- ½ green bell pepper finely chopped
- 1 3.8 oz. can sliced black olives
- 8 oz. package Mexican blend shredded cheese
- ½ cup Jalapeno peppers pickled and deli sliced

The Toppings:
- 1 8 oz. bottle salsa, mild or hot
- 8 oz. sour cream
- ½ cup cilantro finely chopped
- 1 avocado diced

The First Step:
Preheat oven to 400 degrees with rack in middle position.

Preparing the Fish:
Heat large skillet on medium high. When skillet hot, add canola oil to lightly coat bottom. Brown fish cubes on all sides, leaving fish just barely cooked (you want to keep fish soft and moist since you will be putting it in the oven). Add cumin, chili powder, garlic powder, and salt, tossing to mix. Transfer to a dish and set aside.

To Assemble:
Put first layer of tortilla chips in large baking dish that can also be used for serving. Sprinkle one-third of the tomatoes, green peppers, black olives, salmon and jalapenos if using, and cheese. Repeat layers two more times.

Put in oven for around 9 to 10 minutes until cheese is melted. Be careful not to leave in the oven any longer than necessary as the fish will dry out.

Serve with salsa, sour cream, avocados and cilantro to use as toppings.

Cook's Tips:

This is a great afternoon snack when friends come over. You can make it very quickly, especially if everyone helps. As they say, many hands make light work.

Cook's Notes:

This was one of my earliest recipe ideas I wanted to include in my book since teenagers like nachos and using salmon would make it healthier. I had a difficult time conceptualizing how to put it together, and my Aunty Joycelyne gave me some good suggestions. She is an excellent cook, a really nice person, and Uncle Shimo sure is lucky to be married to her.

Aunty Lynn's Salmon Farfalle

Preparation and Cooking Time: 45 minutes
Serves: 4

The Sauce:
- ✿ 1¼ lb. salmon cut into ½" cubes
- ✿ 2 oz. pancetta sliced
- ✿ 1 shallot finely diced
- ✿ 1 small zucchini cut into small cubes
- ✿ 3 Tablespoons olive oil
- ✿ 2 Tablespoons butter
- ✿ 1 teaspoon red pepper flakes
- ✿ Zest and juice of 1 lemon

The Pasta:
- ✿ ¾ lb. dried farfalle

The Garnish:
- ✿ ¼ cup fresh basil leaves chiffonade

The Preparation:

Bring large pot of water to a boil over high heat. Add 2 Tablespoons kosher salt, then add pasta. Stir to keep from sticking together and cook until al dente. Drain in colander and set aside. Reserve pasta water to use later.

Heat large skillet on medium high heat. Add pancetta with 1 Tablespoon olive oil and cook until browned but not crispy. Remove from pan. Heat 2 Tablespoons olive oil in same pan. Salt and pepper salmon cubes. Add salmon to hot oil and cook until just done (about 2 to 3 minutes). Set aside with pancetta. Add butter to pan, then shallot, pepper flakes, lemon juice and zest. When shallots softened, add pancetta, salmon and zucchini to pan. As soon as it comes to temp, add pasta and toss, adding around ¼ cup pasta water to moisten. Remove to serving bowl, toss with basil, and add lemon wedges on the side to finish.

Cook's Tips:

Be sure not to overcook salmon as it will get hard and dry. This happened on my first try. It is also best to serve this dish with fresh lemon wedges on the side to add freshness to the taste.

Cook's Notes:

When I think of salmon, I think of my Aunty Lynn who lives in Seldovia, Alaska. Whenever she comes to visit us, she would always give us salmon, the very best fresh, bottled or smoked salmon I ever tasted. My aunty is an excellent cook. Mom especially talks about her bread making talents. She made the best croissants, any type of breads with any type of flours, bagels – you name it. For years, she was the chef at the school in Seldovia. Mom says she would make fresh hot dog or hamburger buns, and of course, her pizza dough was the best. They made pizza one year for a fundraiser to send the senior class to Portugal. It was a big success. Aunty Lynn can also whip up fresh pasta in a jiffy. That is why I think of her with this salmon and pasta combination.

Cousin Chandra's Shrimp Capellini

Preparation and Cooking Time: 45 minutes
Serves: 4

The Shrimp:
- 1¼ lbs. fresh, uncooked, peeled and deveined shrimp (16-20 per pound size)
- 2 cloves garlic minced
- 1 lemon, zest and juice
- 1 teaspoon red pepper flakes
- 2 cups small cherry tomatoes cut in half
- 5 Tablespoons extra virgin olive oil

For Garnish:
- ¼ cup basil, cut chiffonade
- Lemon wedges

The Pasta:
- ¾ lb. capellini

The First Steps:
Preheat oven to 400 degrees.

Bring large pot filled with water to a boil. Add 2 Tablespoons kosher salt then cook pasta al dente (around 2 to 3 minutes). As soon as pasta ready, drain in colander and retain 1 cup pasta water for later.

To Prepare Shrimp:
While waiting for oven to come up to temperature and water to boil, in a large bowl, toss shrimp with 3 Tablespoons olive oil, tomatoes and ½ teaspoon salt. Spread in one layer on a baking sheet pan and roast in oven for around 6 to 7 minutes or until shrimp just turn pink. As soon as they are pink, remove to a bowl to stop the cooking.

As soon as pasta is done, heat large skillet on medium high. When skillet hot, add 2 Tablespoons olive oil, garlic and red pepper flakes. Be careful not to burn garlic – it should be just toasty and light brown. Add shrimp, lemon juice and zest. Toss to mix, add pasta with some hot pasta water to moisten. Bring up to temperature, then immediately remove to serving dish and garnish with basil.

Cook's Tips:

Serve with lemon wedges on the side. It adds freshness to the pasta when you squeeze fresh lemon juice as you eat. You may substitute mint for the basil. It is just as good. Also, you may substitute one finely diced Serrano pepper (seeds removed) instead of the red pepper flakes. I tried it both ways and each is just as good.

Cook's Notes:

I have not had the opportunity to get to know my cousin Chandra that well because she lives in Ashland, Oregon. When I was much younger, she would come to visit when Aunty Lynn was here and we would go to the beach, but it was only for short periods. What I do know is that she is a really good cook, and she told me on one of her trips about making shrimp capellini at her restaurant. It sounded good, so I decided to experiment with it. Okay Cousin Chandra, here is my version. Let's do a side by side next time you visit Hawaii.

Aunty Jenna's Dungeness Crab Monterey Jack Cheese Omelette

Preparation and Cooking Time: 45 minutes
Serves: 4

The Ingredients:

- ❀ 8 oz. Dungeness crab meat
- ❀ ½ cup scallions, green and white parts, finely chopped
- ❀ 10 large eggs beaten
- ❀ 12 oz. bacon sliced 1/8"
- ❀ 1 cup shredded Monterey Jack cheese

The First Step:

In medium size sauté pan, brown sliced becon. Remove from pan to small dish lined with paper towel to absorb oil. Use paper towels to also remove most of the bacon fat from pan. Add scallions, toss to soften, and remove to same small bowl.

Making the Omelette:

In an omelette pan, heat some canola oil over medium high heat. Mix crab, eggs, bacon and scallions, and when pan comes to temp, add one-fourth mixture to pan. Reduce heat slightly. As the omelette cooks on one side, lift with a spatula and rotate pan to let the uncooked parts run to edges of pan. Add cheese and when the top of the omelette looks almost set, fold over into thirds and remove to plate. Continue same steps for other three omelettes.

Cook's Tips:

This makes a great Sunday brunch. Be sure you break up the Dungeness crab so it won't be too chunky, also so you can find all the shells. The bacon really adds a good flavor here. It is better if you make the bacon really crispy.

Cook's Notes:

My crab omelette is dedicated to my Aunty Jenna because it is very sexy and so is she. When your friends and family eat this omelette, they will know it is one of a kind, just like Aunty Jenna. The crab in the omelette reminds me that Aunty Jenna can be a little crabby at times, but just like Aunty Jenna, this omelette always brings home the bacon. Beware of making this omelette on Sunday morning, or you will be stuck making omelettes every Sunday morning forever.

Daddy's Mini Lasagna with Shrimp

Preparation and Cooking Time: 1½ hours
Serves: 4

The White Sauce:
- 4 Tablespoons butter
- 4 Tablespoons flour
- 3 cups 1% milk
- 1 cup Carnation milk (do not use low fat version)
- Freshly ground black pepper
- 1½ teaspoons kosher salt

The Shrimp:
- 1¼ lb. cleaned and deveined fresh shrimp, finely chopped
- 2 Tablespoons butter
- 1 Tablespoon olive oil
- 3 Tablespoons scallions, finely chopped
- 1 large or 2 small zucchini, finely diced
- 1½ teaspoons kosher salt
- Freshly ground black pepper
- 8 ounces fresh mozzarella grated
- 1 cup parmesan reggiano freshly grated
- 1 package won ton wrappers

The First Step:
Preheat oven to 375 degrees. Use a 9x13 baking dish.

Making the Sauce:
Preheat small pot, then add 2 tablespoons butter. When butter melted, add flour and mix well until smooth. Add milk slowly, mixing constantly. Keep on medium low heat mixing continuously until sauce thickens (around 5 minutes). When thickened, add Carnation milk and remove from heat.

Making the Shrimp:
Heat medium size skillet with 2 tablespoons butter and 1 Tablespoon olive oil on medium heat. When skillet hot, add shrimp and green onions. As soon as shrimp turns pink, remove from heat, add zucchini, salt and pepper. Transfer to a bowl.

The Assembly:
Put 1 cup of the white sauce on bottom of dish. You are going to be making individual stacks, 3 layers high. Start by putting first layer of won ton wrappers over sauce on bottom of baking dish. Top each one with the shrimp mixture, then sprinkle with mozzarella and parmesan. Cover each stack with another wrapper, topped with sauce, followed by shrimp mixture, mozzarella and parmesan. For last layer, just cover won top wrapper with sauce and finish with grated parmesan.

Cover baking dish with foil and bake for 30 to 35 minutes until bubbly. Remove foil, turn oven to broil and brown top before taking out (should take around 3 minutes).

To Plate:

Let rest for around 5 minutes, then place the individual stacks on plates to serve. You can top with basil cut chiffonade style.

Cook's Tips:

The first time I made this dish, it turned out a little dry, therefore I discovered if you add more milk to thin out the sauce, it helps. You definitely want the sauce on the thin side to allow for absorption and baking time. You must use fresh shrimp, and not any that have been brined. Be very, very careful not to overcook shrimp and definitely take off the heat before adding the zucchini because you don't want the zucchini to be mushy since you will also be baking this dish.

Cook's Notes:

My Daddy is a fanatic when it comes to canned Carnation milk! The way he uses it is almost religious. He uses it in his tea, his oatmeal, for Mommy's coffee and even drinks it straight out of the can. I figured I had to make something that included his beloved Carnation milk, so thus this recipe was born.

If it wasn't for my Dad, this cookbook would never have happened. My Daddy always gives me so much encouragement and praise. We are alike in so many ways – we both have ADD, dyslexia, love to eat then need to work hard to burn off the excess. When I first started to cook, he loved my food. Then he wanted me to cook when he invited friends over. He would brag about how good I was. Then he came up with this cookbook idea and made it happen by finding Dennis Lowery. I am the luckiest girl on this planet being with my Dad!

Aunty Lynette's
Mexican Seared Ahi Salad

Preparation and Cooking Time: 1 hour
Serves: 4

The Vinaigrette:
- 1 garlic clove halved
- 1 teaspoon Dijon mustard
- ¼ cup Pomegranate vinegar
- 1 teaspoon honey
- 1/3 cup olive oil
- Kosher salt and freshly ground pepper to taste

The Cherry Tomato Salsa:
- 1 basket cherry tomatoes, quartered
- ½ cup red onion finely diced
- 1 jalapeno seeded and minced
- ½ lemon juiced

- ¼ cup fresh cilantro chopped
- ¼ teaspoon kosher salt

The Salad:
- 4 small red potatoes
- 4 eggs
- ¼ lb. haricot verts or sugar snap peas
- 1 package mixed baby salad greens
- ½ cup seedless black olives halved

The Fish:
- 4 fresh sushi quality tuna steaks
- 1 package Taco seasoning

Making the Vinaigrette:
Combine all ingredients in a jar. Screw the cap on the jar and shake the vinaigrette vigorously to emulsify. Set aside.

Making the Salsa:
Combine all ingredients in a small bowl. Mix well and set aside.

Making the Salad:
Cook the potatoes and eggs in the same pot. Add water to cover, pinch of salt, and bring to a boil over medium high heat. Once water starts to boil, reduce heat to low and simmer for about 15 minutes. Remove eggs and continue to cook potatoes for another 10 minutes or until done. When the eggs have cooled, shell and cut into quarters, then set aside. Remove the potatoes and add the green beans for about 2 - 3 minutes or until color turns dark green. Be sure not to overcook the beans because you want the beans to be crunchy and have texture. As soon as the beans are done, throw into a bowl of ice water.

Making the Fish:

Rub the fish steaks with olive oil and coat with the taco seasoning. Heat a grill pan over medium high heat. Add about 2 Tablespoons of olive oil to the pan when hot. Sear the tuna steaks for about 2 minutes on each side. Transfer tuna to a cutting board, let rest for a couple minutes, then slice.

Assembling the Salad:

Cut the potatoes into quarters. In a large bowl, combine the potatoes, beans, olives and salad greens. Drizzle the salad with the vinaigrette to coat. Toss very gently because you don't want to break up the potatoes and bruise the greens. Put the tossed salad down either on a serving platter or individual plates. Arrange the seared ahi on the salad greens, top with the salsa, and finish with the eggs around the rim.

Cook's Tips:

It is really important to use sushi grade tuna steaks, and it is even more important not to overcook them. The first time I seared the ahi steaks, they turned out medium well. You want it medium rare. A trick is to observe the side of the steak as it cooks. As soon as you see the color change on at least one-fourth from the bottom up, turn the steak. It is done when you see the color changed one-fourth on the second side.

Cook's Notes:

My Aunty Lynette is the ultimate salad maker. Whenever we had a family dinner, she would make the salad and it was always delicious. She would use ingredients I never tasted before like jicama that I really learned to enjoy. She also made the best sticky rice, better than any restaurant. My Aunty Lynette owns the upscale tea kiosk on the third floor at the Ala Moana Shopping Center. It is called the Pacific Place Tea Garden. She has also created some unique tea sorbets that are sold at Whole Foods. The flavors are dragon phoenix jasmine pearl, passionberry, mango, pineapple, lychee, hibiscus orange tisane, and she has some teas flavored gelatos like matcha green tea and hojicha. My favorites are the green tea and lychee.

Mihye's Seafood Medley Somen Salad

Preparation and Cooking Time: 45 minutes
Serves: 4

The Vinaigrette:
- 1 teaspoon sesame oil
- 3 Tablespoons light soy sauce
- 3 Tablespoons sugar
- 2 Tablespoons rice wine vinegar
- 1 Tablespoon lemon juice plus 1 Tablespoon zest
- ¼ teaspoon kosher salt
- 3 Tablespoons canola oil

The Salad:
- 10 oz. package dried somen noodle
- ½ head iceberg lettuce finely shredded
- 1 Japanese cucumber julienned
- 1 package radish sprouts
- ¾ cup Cilantro, leaves only
- 8 pieces fresh shrimp, size 16-20
- 4 large scallops
- 8 oz. lump Dungeness crabmeat

First Steps:
Bring large pot of water to a boil over high heat. Add somen noodles to pot and cook about 1 minute. Drain in colander and immediately immerse in ice bath until ready to assemble salad.

Bring medium pot filled halfway with water to a boil. Add shrimp and scallops. As soon as shrimp turns pink (around 1½ minutes), transfer shrimp and scallops to another ice bath. Once cool, dry with paper towel and set aside.

Assembling the Salad:
Divide somen noodles among four plates. Top each with one-fourth of the other ingredients, arranging each one separately around the sides of the somen. Drizzle with dressing.

Cook's Tips:

For vinaigrette, you can substitute lime instead of lemon. I like both and can't decide which I liked better. They are both good.

Cook's Notes:

Mihye is another friend that is fun to be with. She is quite "out of the box". We were in ceramics class together and making vases. Her vase had a face in the style of pop art with eyes that were uneven and huge lips. I thought it was crazy good! Many afternoons, we hang together while waiting for pickup and just talk, watch anime videos, or study. I named this dish after her because she is tall and skinny and eats salad, and I wanted the salad to be Asian.

Mommy's Baked Salmon

Preparation and Cooking Time: 1½ hours
Serves: 6

The Salmon:
- ❀ 2 salmon fillets skin on
- ❀ 2 round onions thinly sliced
- ❀ 2 large lemons thinly sliced
- ❀ l block butter
- ❀ 1 lb. bacon
- ❀ Kosher salt
- ❀ Freshly ground black pepper
- ❀ Heavy duty aluminum foil

The Dressing:
- ❀ 1 cup mayonnaise
- ❀ 1 cup sour cream
- ❀ ¼ cup fresh dill chopped
- ❀ ¼ cup cornichons finely chopped
- ❀ 2 Tablespoons capers

The First Step:
Preheat oven to 400 degrees.

To Prepare:
Cut foil with enough length to fully wrap salmon. Salt and pepper both pieces of salmon. Lay one salmon piece, skin side down, on foil. Layer completely with sliced onions and then sliced lemons. Cover with bacon slices and dot with butter. Cover with other salmon piece, skin side up, and repeat steps. Wrap tightly with foil leaving foil ends facing up so juices will not escape when salmon is cooking. Bake around 1 hour, 15 minutes.

To Serve:
Remove salmon from foil, basting the fish with the dripping. Serve with dressing on the side.

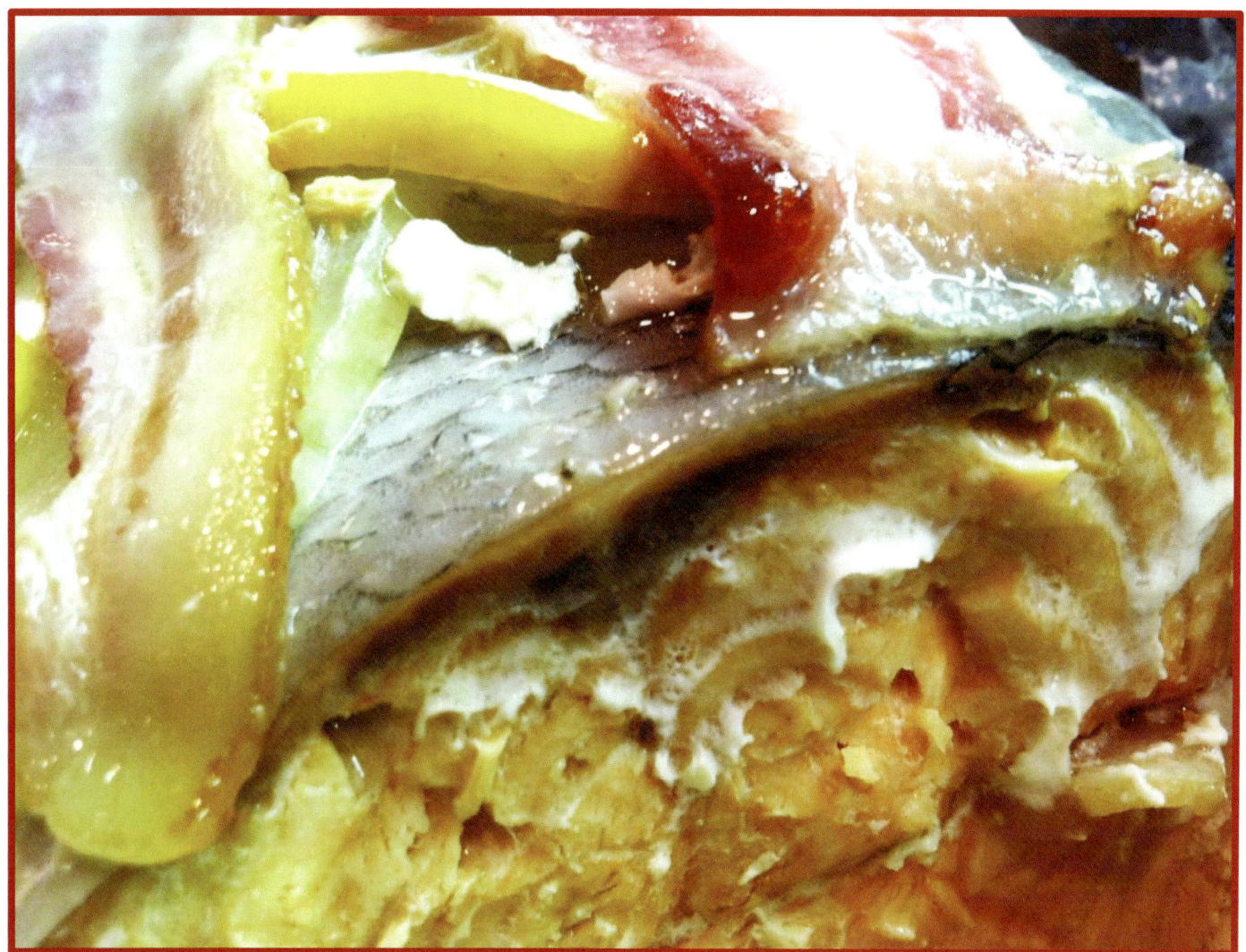

Cook's Tips:

This recipe is another one that is fast, easy, and no fail. The cooking time may vary depending on the thickness of the salmon. When you take it out, open the foil wrapping, and press down on the salmon. It will be firm if done. If it is still soft, bake it longer. It is important that the salmon and onions are cooked, and it is also important to baste with the drippings. Make a tarter sauce to serve with it. Also, a wild rice mixture like Uncle Ben's goes well with this dish.

Cook's Notes:

Whenever Mom made this, it was always so good. I wanted to make it one day, so I asked her to teach me. This recipe was passed on to my Mom by Popo, and Popo learned to make it from a family friend. Now, I can keep the tradition going and pass this on to my child.

Popo's Shrimp Curry
(Popo is Grandmother in Chinese)

Preparation and Cooking Time: 1 hour
Serves: 4

The Shrimp:
- 1½ lbs. peeled and deveined fresh shrimp (16-20 size)
- 2 bay leaves
- ½ lemon sliced thin

The Curry Sauce:
- 1 small green bell pepper finely chopped
- 1 small onion finely chopped
- 2 stalks celery finely chopped
- 5 Tablespoons butter
- 3½ Tablespoons flour
- 3 Tablespoons curry powder

- 3 cups milk or more as needed
- ½ cup canned coconut milk
- 2 teaspoons kosher salt
- ¼ teaspoon white pepper

The Garnishes:
- Rice, cooked (can be white, brown, or long grain)
- ¾ pound bacon, cooked crisp and chopped
- 3 hardboiled eggs, finely chopped
- Italian parsley finely chopped (optional)

To Prepare Shrimp:
Bring medium size pot of water with bay leaves and lemon to a boil (you should have enough water to cover shrimp). Add shrimp and cook only until shrimp turns pink (around 2 minutes). Put into a colander to drain water. Set aside.

To Prepare Curry Sauce:
Heat large skillet on medium heat. When pan comes to temp, add butter, green peppers, onion and celery. Cook until vegetables cooked through and soft (be careful to not caramelize or brown vegetables). This should take around 10 minutes. Add curry powder and stir through. Add flour, mix into vegetables, and cook for another 5 minutes. Add milk (save coconut milk for last), shrimp, salt and pepper, bringing up temp to just below boiling. Add coconut milk, bring up to serving temperature, and remove from heat. Do not bring to up to boiling temperature and do not leave on the heat because of milk. If serving to be delayed, do not add coconut milk until ready to serve. Bring curry mixture back up to temperature, add coconut milk, then serve.

To Plate:
Place a scoop of rice on a plate or shallow bowl. Cover with a serving of the curry. Garnish with bacon, egg and parsley.

Cook's Tips:
You must use fresh shrimp that is NOT BRINED. One time when I made this dish, the shrimp was brined and we could not eat it because the shrimp was too salty. It is really important not to caramelize the vegetables as this will change the flavor and be sure to cook the raw flour taste out before adding milk. For the topping, do not skip the bacon and chopped egg, but if you do not like parsley, you can skip that.

Cook's Notes:
My Popo was the best grandmother anyone could have. She taught me a lot of different things, like making apple pie, muffins, pancakes, and arranging flowers. Mom says this was Popo's signature dish. Whenever she had company and needed to make something special for lunch or dinner, she always made shrimp curry and served it with her fantastic mango chutney. I want other people to share the joy that I have had eating this dish.

Uncle Pat's Baked Salmon with Potato Stuffing

Preparation and Cooking Time: 1½ hours
Serves: 4

The Salmon:
- 4 salmon fillets
- 4 Tablespoons butter brought to room temperature
- 2 Tablespoons lemon zest
- 4 fresh dill sprigs
- 2 Tablespoons capers
- 2 Tablespoons finely chopped Italian parsley

The Potato:
- 2 russet potatoes cut into large cubes
- 1 small zucchini diced
- ¾ cup sour cream
- ½ cup milk
- 1 Tablespoon butter
- ½ teaspoon salt, ¼ for cooking potatoes and ¼ for later

The First Step:
Preheat oven to 350 degrees.

To Prepare Potatoes:
In small pot, add cut up potatoes and ¼ teaspoon salt with enough water to cover potatoes. Bring pot to a boil then lower heat and simmer around 15 minutes until potatoes cooked. While potatoes are cooking, finely dice the zucchini and set aside. When potatoes are done, drain in a colander and return to pot. Mash potatoes with a masher or fork, then add zucchini and butter. Mix together so heat of potatoes start to cook zucchini. Add sour cream, milk and ¼ teaspoon salt.

To Prepare Salmon:
Combine the butter, lemon zest, parsley and capers. Slit the middle of each salmon fillet to make as big a pocket as possible and stuff pocket with the mashed potato mixture. Lightly season the top and bottom of the salmon with salt and freshly ground pepper, then put one-fourth of the butter mixture and a dill sprig on top. Wrap each salmon piece with parchment paper, making a tight seal to retain the juices as the salmon cooks. Bake for about 20 to 25 minutes.

Cook's Notes:
This one is fun to make because of the assembly. Like the other baked salmon recipe, you have to be sure it cooks long enough so the salmon is cooked and the mashed potatoes in the center very warm. The good part about this dish is that it is a complete meal and all you need is a salad on the side.

Cook's Notes:
I just love hanging out with my Uncle Pat. We always have so much fun together and he takes me to many different places like the movies, Dave & Busters, the beach, and whenever I sleep over on Saturday night, on Sunday he would make scrambled eggs, Portuguese sausage and rice for breakfast. Uncle Pat loves his fish, including the head and eyeballs. He demolishes the fish head – it is only a stack of bones when he finishes. Mom says when they were young, Uncle Pat was the mashed potato king. He really liked mashed potatoes and would put a big pile on his plate, digging a hole in the middle and filling it with gravy. So Uncle Pat, I combined the two, fish and mashed potatoes, just for you!

Uncle Neil's Hoisin Salmon Burger

Preparation and Cooking Time: 1½ hours
Serves: 4

The Marinade:
- ❊ 4 Tablespoons hoisin sauce
- ❊ 1 Tablespoon fresh ginger minced
- ❊ 2 garlic cloves minced
- ❊ 1 Tablespoon Shaoxing wine (Chinese rice wine)
- ❊ ¼ teaspoon Coleman dry mustard
- ❊ 1 Tablespoon light soy sauce
- ❊ 1 teaspoon toasted sesame oil
- ❊ ½ teaspoon kosher salt

The Ingredients:
- ❊ 1¼ lbs. fresh salmon fillet
- ❊ 4 hamburger buns
- ❊ 4 slices tomato
- ❊ 1 package baby spinach leaves

The Burger Spread:
- ❊ 1 cup mayonnaise
- ❊ ½ cup cilantro finely chopped
- ❊ 2 Tablespoons fresh lime juice

The First Step:
Combine marinade ingredients together in medium size bowl. Prepare salmon by removing skin, cutting 4 individual pieces, and removing any pin bones. Marinate for 45 minutes.

Making the Burger:
Heat large skillet on medium high heat. When pan hot, add 3 Tablespoons canola oil and fry salmon pieces until just done. Set aside. Toast hamburger bun halves in a large skillet.

The Assembly:
Put general amount of spread on the buns. Mound with salmon, slice of tomato and spinach.

Cooks Tips:

This burger tastes better if the buns are toasted well and the salmon nicely seared on the outside but just cooked on the inside. When I first tried this recipe, I used lemon juice with half of the spread and lime juice for the other half. Lime tasted way better. I also cut the tomato slices very thin, but thicker slices were better the second time.

Cook's Notes:

I think of Uncle Neil with my hoisin salmon burger. The presentation is very pleasing to the eye, the flavor combination a little complex with a surprising punch from the lime juice, and reminds me of a mad scientist with the number of marinade ingredients. When Uncle cooks, especially with his Asian flavors for ribs, he uses around 20 ingredients. He once tried to tell us what he used – past ten, we went unconscious.

As a lunchtime meal, this hoisin burger gets the job done, which of course is the bottom line when it comes to Uncle Neil. He is an attorney by profession, a photographer by avocation, an athlete when it comes to golf and tennis, and a handyman/repairman in his free time. It takes two hands to handle this burger, and Aunty Carole will tell you it takes three to handle Uncle Neil!

Sensei George's Poached Salmon Tofu Salad

Preparation Time: 45 minutes
Serves: 4

The Dressing:
- 4 Tablespoons light soy sauce
- 2 Tablespoons lemon juice
- 3 Tablespoons canola oil
- 2 Tablespoons mirin
- 2 teaspoons sugar
- 2 teaspoons toasted sesame oil
- 2 teaspoons Ko-chu-jang (Korean hot bean paste)
- 4 teaspoons toasted sesame seeds
- 1 teaspoon red chili flakes
- 2 scallions finely chopped

The Salmon:
- 1 lb. fresh salmon cut into 4 pieces
- 2 lemon slices

The Tofu:
- 1 20 oz. tofu block
- ½ cup cornstarch

The Salad:
- 1 package baby greens, spring mix, or baby lettuce

The Garnishes:
- ½ Japanese cucumber julienned
- ½ cup cilantro finely chopped

Making the Salmon:
Bring pan filled with 2" water to boil. Add lemon slices, 2 teaspoons kosher salt., and salmon pieces. Turn to low heat and poach for 8 to10 minutes. When done, remove to a paper towel lined dish to absorb the water.

Making the Tofu:
Wrap the tofu block with paper towels to absorb as much of the moisture as you can, then cut block into 4 pieces. Heat pan on medium heat until hot. Add 2 Tablespoons canola oil. Coat tofu with cornstarch and fry until lightly browned. Remove to a dish and set aside.

To Plate the Salad:
Put a serving of salad greens on each plate. Place tofu on the greens, then salmon on tofu. Mix the cucumber and cilantro together and add a heaping Tablespoon on top of each salmon. Dress salad and serve immediately.

Cook's Tips:

You don't want to overcook the salmon, so be careful to simmer and not boil in the water. Since tofu is so fragile, it is easier to hold the tofu piece in your left hand and pat on the cornstarch on each side instead of trying to dip or roll the tofu in the cornstarch. Any extra dressing can be placed in a bowl and brought to the table in case anyone would like to add more dressing.

Cook's Notes:

Sensei George Kotaka is my karate instructor. I am extremely fortunate and blessed to be studying under him for the past seven years. Sensei George is very disciplined and dedicated, and he is also kind and compassionate. I have learned not only karate but I also learned the qualities of discipline, perseverance, how to strive for excellence, and how to always do the best you can because these traits are personified in Sensei George. I also learned the lesson of disappointment in myself when I did not put out my best and he strongly let me know it by ending the lesson early.

I was age 11 when I started studying under Sensei George. I was uncoordinated and very insecure. Karate helped me build physical strength, coordination, and self-confidence, but being able to share with Sensei George during our sessions taught me some important life lessons. His character, actions, beliefs, accomplishments and ethics helped me grow as a person.

Aunty Laura's Fish Cake Patties

Preparation and Cooking Time: 1½ hours
Serves: 4

The Patty:

- 6 oz. fresh salmon fillet, finely chopped
- 10 oz. fresh halibut or mahimahi fillet, finely chopped
- 2 Tablespoons scallions, finely chopped
- ¼ cup red bell pepper, finely chopped
- ¼ cup celery, finely chopped (optional)
- ½ cup mayonnaise
- 1 egg, lightly beaten
- ½ teaspoon Dijon mustard
- 1 teaspoon kosher salt
- Freshly ground black pepper
- 1/8 teaspoon garlic powder
- 1/8 teaspoon paprika
- 2 dashes hot sauce like Frank's Red Hot or Tabasco
- 2 cups Panko (Japanese bread crumbs) for coating

The Sauce:

- ¾ cup mayonnaise
- 2 Tablespoons ketchup
- 2 Tablespoons Cornichons minced
- 2 Tablespoons cilantro, finely chopped
- 2 teaspoons lime juice and 1 teaspoon lime zest
- Dash of hot sauce

The Garnish:

- Lime wedges
- Cilantro leaves

Making the Patty:

To prepare the patties, combine all the ingredients except for the Panko in a small bowl. Mix well. Form into six cakes. Coat the cakes with Panko and refrigerate for about 45 minutes.

Heat large skillet over medium high heat, add olive oil and fry patties until golden brown, turning only once. It will take around 2½ to 3 minutes per side.

Plating the Patty:

Make a pool of sauce on the bottom of the plate and place a patty on the sauce. Garnish with a lime wedge and some cilantro leaves.

Cook's Tips:

Since these patties are loose and hard to handle, I find it easier to coat them with Panko if you hold a patty in your left hand and sprinkle the Panko with your right hand. Put the patty Panko side down on the holding dish, then sprinkle and pat down Panko on the topside. This way, the patties don't break up. It is really important to not overheat your skillet, otherwise the patties will burn and the inside will not be cooked. If your pan is too hot, remove it from the heat, cool it down and then start over to reheat skillet. You can choose to omit the celery. I included celery because my Dad loves celery. Absolutely use the lime wedge to finish – a squeeze of lime gives the patty a real fresh taste.

Cook's Notes:

Aunty Laura gave me my very first cookbook when I was 8 years old. It was a cookbook for kids that had a lot of fun baking recipes like cookies with easy to follow instructions. Later, she gave me a book with easy recipes that took only a few steps to make. She knew I liked to cook, took inspiration from my Aunty Carole, and wanted to encourage me by giving me these easy to read, easy to follow recipes. When I think of Aunty Laura, I picture a huge smile and hear her hearty, happy happy laugh.

"March Hare"

"My March Hare is the archetypical proper British hare wearing a formal British racing green (BRG) coat and tails being at the tea party exactly at 4:00, showing proper disgust for the White Rabbit not being there on time. The pocket watch in his hand shows 4:00 which would normally be 5:00 on any other watch, except not in Wonderland."

Vegetarian

Catherine's Cheese Manicotti

Preparation and Cooking Time: 1½ hours
Serves: 4

The Sauce:
- ❧ 1 25 oz. bottle Tomato Basil pasta sauce
- ❧ 1 5.5 oz. can V-8 juice
- ❧ 1 handful fresh basil torn

The Crepes:
- ❧ 1 cup Bisquick
- ❧ ¾ cup plus 1Tablespoon 1% milk
- ❧ 2 eggs

The Filling:
- ❧ 3 cups ricotta
- ❧ 2 large eggs
- ❧ ½ cup grated Parmesan reggiano
- ❧ ¼ cup chopped Italian parsley
- ❧ ½ teaspoon kosher salt
- ❧ Freshly ground black pepper
- ❧ ½ pound fresh mozzarella cut into sticks ¼" thick

The First Step:
Preheat oven to 425 degrees with oven rack in the middle position.

Making the Sauce:
Heat pasta sauce in pan on medium heat. When heated, add tomato juice and basil. Cook on low heat until basil is cooked through (around 5 minutes).

Making the Crepes:
To make crepes, beat eggs in a bowl with a fork. Add milk and Bisquick. Mix well to get lumps out. Heat small non-stick skillet over medium heat. When heated, brush pan with butter. Drop 2 Tablespoons batter into skillet. Immediately rotate until batter covers bottom. Use spatula around edges to loosen. Cook until underside is slightly brown (around 30 seconds). Invert crepe onto a clean towel. Repeat until you have a total of 12 crepes.

Making the Filling:
Stir together filling ingredients except for mozzarella.

To Assemble:
Spread 1½ cups sauce in 9x13 ceramic baking dish. On a work surface, lay crepe browned side up, spreading ¼ cup filling in a line across center, and top with a mozzarella strip. Fold into thirds with top and bottom overlapping to enclose filling, leaving sides open. Put seam side down in baking dish. Repeat, arranging crepes snugly in one layer. Top with rest of sauce. Cover with foil and bake for 25 minutes or until bubbly.

Serve with remaining sauce on the side.

Cook's Tips:

The first time I tried to make a Manicotti recipe, because of the crepes, it was really labor intensive. In fact, the crepes were a disaster – broken, crumpled, burnt, but the taste was good. I kept thinking about it but did not want to go through all that trouble again. That was when I thought of Bisquick. I love using Bisquick. I use it all the time for pancakes and waffles, and I make the best biscuits with it (at least that's what Mom and Dad tell me). Now, I can make this anytime because it is so easy with Bisquick, the ultimate power ingredient that you can use to make just about anything without fail.

Cook's Notes:

This dish is like comfort food. It makes me think of my friend Catherine who is like a big sister to me at school, always there to comfort me. This dish is rolled up and warm and comfy on the inside just like her. Catherine is the responsible one in our group, or should I say, the most mature. She usually has to calm Jasmine and me down because our antics can get too crazy. Sometimes, she is like a big sister to Jasmine because Jasmine spends a lot of time at Catherine's house, and Catherine takes care of Jasmine. Jasmine spends so much time there it's like her second home. She even leaves her socks there. Catherine is a real good cook. Many times, she cooks for the family. She mostly cooks Asian and sometimes Italian. When Jasmine is over, she cooks Mexican, of course.

Aunty Ruby's Beet Ravioli

Preparation and Cooking Time: 2 hours
Serves 4

The Ravioli:
- 1 large beet or 2 smaller ones
- 1 medium russet potato
- ½ cup ricotta cheese
- ½ teaspoon kosher salt
- Freshly ground black pepper
- 1 Tablespoon plain breadcrumbs or Panko
- 1 package won ton wrappers (40 wrappers)

The Sauce:
- ¼ cup butter
- 2 teaspoons poppy seeds

The Garnish:
- ½ cup freshly grated parmesan reggiano

The First Step:
Preheat oven to 350 degrees.

Preparing the Beets:
Wrap beet and potato separately in foil and place on baking sheet. Bake for about 1 hour (beet may be done ahead of potato). When done, remove foil. When cool, peel beet and potato and grate into a medium sized bowl. Add ricotta, salt and pepper. Mix and stir in breadcrumbs.

Making the Raviolis:
Bring large pot of water to a boil.

Have a small dish of water on work surface. Lay won ton wrapper down. Place 1 Tablespoon beet mixture in center, moisten all sides with water, then place another won ton wrapper on top. Push out as much air as possible and seal the edges. Repeat with other won ton wrappers. You should be able to make 20 ravioli.

Start heating large skillet on medium heat. Working in batches, add 1 Tablespoon butter and ¼ teaspoon poppy seeds to pan. Put 6 ravioli in boiling water, stirring frequently. When ravioli floats to surface, remove with slotted spoon and transfer to skillet. Toss ravioli to coat with butter and poppy seeds then remove to a dish. Repeat steps until all ravioli cooked. You will need to work quickly so that ravioli does not get cold.

To Plate:
You can either plate individually or on one large serving platter. Sprinkle with parmesan cheese.

Cook's Tips:

This recipe is time consuming in the preparation but fast in the cooking. Once you have all the ravioli made, it is basically into a pot of hot water until they float to the surface (which only takes a couple minutes), and into a pan of butter. It is best to do it simultaneously so the ravioli on all the plates or in the serving dish are still relatively hot. The first time I made this dish, I did not include the potato. I found the filling was missing something, so the next time I added the potato and liked it much better.

Cook's Notes:

Whenever I grate beets, they come out in little curls that reminds me of Aunty Ruby's hair. Just like her hair, they are short and curly. Also, the color of beets match her name, and when I eat them, they are sweet just like her! Aunty Ruby is the most "go to" person if you need anything. She moves so fast, she is the Energizer Bunny or her other name is Road Runner. When I decided I wanted to make brownies and chocolate chip cookies for a Bake Sale at school, Aunty Ruby found the clear bags and made labels with my name on it, like Cal's Brownies or Cal's Cookies. The packaging looked so good, when the sale started, my brownies and cookies flew out the door, they sold so quickly. It was presentation, presentation, presentation (Aunty Carole's mantra) and Aunty Ruby!

Uncle Dennis' Deconstructed Eggplant Parmigiana

Preparation and Cooking Time: 1½ hours
Serves: 6

The Eggplant:
- 3 medium eggplants cut into ¼" rounds

The Tomato Sauce:
- 1 26 oz. bottle tomato basil sauce

The Ricotta Sauce:
- 1 15 oz. ricotta
- ½ lb, fresh mozzarella diced into tiny cubes
- 2/3 cup grated parmesan reggiano

- ¼ cup milk
- ½ teaspoon salt
- Fresh ground black pepper
- ¼ cup fresh basil chiffonade

The Topping:
- ¾ cup Panko
- 1 Tablespoon olive oil
- ¼ cup grated parmesan reggiano
- 1/8 cup Italian parsley finely chopped

The First Step:
Preheat oven to 350 degrees. You will need a 9x13 baking dish.

Making the Eggplant:
Heat large pan on medium high heat. When hot, add olive oil to about ¼" deep. Cook the eggplant slices, around 2 minutes each side until nicely browned. Transfer cooked eggplant slices to paper towels to drain. Add more olive oil to continue cooking the rest of the eggplants.

Making the Ricotta Sauce:
In a small bowl, mix together ricotta and milk until smooth, then add rest of the ingredients.

The Assembly:
Put one-third of the eggplant on the bottom of the baking dish, then top with one-third of the tomato sauce. Follow with dollops of the ricotta sauce. You should use about one-third of the ricotta using your fingers to slightly flatten. Repeat with two more layers of the same.

Making the Topping:
Heat pan on medium heat. Add olive oil and Panko to pan and remove to dish when Panko is light brown. Mix in parmesan and parsley, then sprinkle over top of baking dish.

The Final Step:

Bake for around 35 to 45 minutes until eggplant is bubbly. Remove from oven and let rest for 5 to 10 minutes before serving.

Cook's Tips:

One of the times I made this dish, I put too much of the ricotta sauce between the layers because I didn't want to waste it. The dish turned out to be a white, goopy mess. Don't worry about using all – just use what looks to be a good balance between the ricotta and tomato sauce.

Cook's Notes:

Thank you, Uncle Dennis, for bringing my cookbook to life. I am so glad my Dad found you, and I am so glad I cooked for you because that is why this cookbook was born that evening when you ate my eggplant parmigiana and really liked it. I think you liked my risotto and meatballs also, but it was the eggplant that sealed it. This is a different version of what I made for you that night. I have practiced and experimented, and I think you will like this one more! This one is like a combination of a gratin and an eggplant parmesan. I like it better because the flavors are all separate – the eggplant, the sauce, and the crispy topping which normally would be the coating for the eggplant slices and get soggy. This way, it stays crunchy – as Martin Yan says, "texture contrast".

My Uncle Dennis lives in Florida, and one year, we all met up in Richmond, Virginia. While there, he treated us to dinner at an elegant Italian restaurant. He and Dad told the chef I was writing a cookbook and that, since I loved Italian food, there would be many Italian dishes in my book. The chef made some special dishes for us to try which were absolutely delicious, and we were so full after that meal. It was one of the most memorable restaurant dinners I ever ate. Whenever I make this dish, I think of Uncle Dennis and the good times we had when we met up in Richmond, Virginia.

"Walrus"

"My Walrus, eating an oyster while crying and holding a handkerchief in his hand to mop up his tears, is really a poem. Just to remind you, 'the time has come the Walrus said, to speak of many things, of shoes, of ships, of sealing wax, of cabbages and kings, and why the sea is boiling hot, and whether pigs have wings'."

To all my friends and family... If your name wasn't included in this book, please stay tuned for the second...

CPSIA information can be obtained
at www.ICGtesting.com
Printed in the USA
LVIC01n1424051013
355372LV00002B